TO THE SOUL

A SHORT COLLECTION OF POEMS

ARPITA CHOWDHURY

Copyright © Arpita Chowdhury
All Rights Reserved.

This book has been self-published with all reasonable efforts taken to make the material error-free by the author. No part of this book shall be used, reproduced in any manner whatsoever without written permission from the author, except in the case of brief quotations embodied in critical articles and reviews.

The Author of this book is solely responsible and liable for its content including but not limited to the views, representations, descriptions, statements, information, opinions and references ["Content"]. The Content of this book shall not constitute or be construed or deemed to reflect the opinion or expression of the Publisher or Editor. Neither the Publisher nor Editor endorse or approve the Content of this book or guarantee the reliability, accuracy or completeness of the Content published herein and do not make any representations or warranties of any kind, express or implied, including but not limited to the implied warranties of merchantability, fitness for a particular purpose. The Publisher and Editor shall not be liable whatsoever for any errors, omissions, whether such errors or omissions result from negligence, accident, or any other cause or claims for loss or damages of any kind, including without limitation, indirect or consequential loss or damage arising out of use, inability to use, or about the reliability, accuracy or sufficiency of the information contained in this book.

Made with ❤ on the Notion Press Platform
www.notionpress.com

This one is for my dadu... (paternal grandfather)

Contents

Preface

'To the Soul' is an ode to the plethora of emotions one experiences but never really expresses outwardly. I don't remember exactly when I started writing poetry but now it is my comfort zone. I have always felt that poetry has the power to say many things that often remain unsaid. This collection of poems depicts different phases of my heart and my self. An amalgamation of highs and lows. I feel poetry has a language of its own. I hope my readers will be able to connect with the thought and will relate with some of these emotions.

Prologue

How do you define life? Is it like a river or a mountain? Tell me...

1. Emptiness

Have you ever looked at a wall?
Does it feel empty?
Is it hollow?
Perhaps, we would never know.
A chatter, I can hear
A scream muffled
Is it me or someone else?
I wonder.
Many questions to ask,
To whom, that's not certain.
World seems shattering
A domino effect of sorts.
I laugh, I eat, I watch my favorite show
I don't know if this is a denial
"I'm fine" is the least I desire
My nights feel safe, I wish it never ended
Something pricks me
Asks me to give up,
But I know, I won't
How long? I'm not sure
Maybe it's just overthinking
Anyways! Tell me one thing.
What does emptiness feel like?

2. I do

The blooming rose looks at me
I look for peace, perhaps that's rare
At the center, I stand
At the center, I fall
Rising from the ashes,
A golden streak of hope,
Things falls apart,
Yet my hope does not
A world full of chaotic currents,
The web of darkness cannot hold
Upright do I stand--
No wind can knock me down
Hollowness hasn't yet engulfed me,
Dawn follows Dusk,
Happiness or gloom
It is all the same
I do hope to bounce back
I do.

3. Leave

No, I'm not perfect.
No one is.
What if I leave abruptly?
What if sentences only have commas?
Let's come back to nowhere
Let there be no question
They seem fine
I'm not.
A small tap is all you need,
Entering a cyclone it seems,
An endless sleep
With collapsing dreams
The heart is pounding
Reasons are uncertain
Close you eyes!
What do you see?
Complete oblivion,
I gather.
Is leaving an option?
Is holding on a possibility?
I doubt.
I doubt.
I doubt.

4. I remember you

Your words,
Your thoughts,
Your ideas,
I remember everything
To the core of my heart.
You have been around,
since forever,
You still remain,
Like a soft feather.
A lot to share,
A lot to talk about,
I know you can hear,
That connect is clear.
You see me from far away,
I know you do,
Let me feel your strength,
Let me remember you,
A sunshine forever.

5. We never forget

We never forget,
That fading touch,
Memories within,
Reeling back again...
Endless laughter,
Warmth of the heart,
Time never stops,
but-- we wish it did.
We never forget,
The departed is not lost because
We never forget…

6. Can you hear me?

Is there light on the other side?
Gasping for breath, I ask.
Loads to say, not a word to utter,
I scream and scream
Nobody to hear,
A noise within,
Something's slipping off
I don't know what
I'm smiling
Yet a hollowness engulfs
I don't feel myself
Not anymore
Its crumbling down,
You see me as normal?
Perhaps, I am.
Or am I not?
Who knows?
Vanishing is an option?
Do you know what it feels like?
Do you understand me?
Can you see me?
Perhaps, I sleep now.
Perhaps, forever.

7. Can't

My steps don't move anymore,
All thoughts are blocked
I can't think clearly
A haze crops up
I don't have answers
Happiness is temporary
Can't face the faces
Can't speak anymore
Hiding, hiding and hiding
Running to places I don't know
Sitting at a place
Where no one can see me
How will I escape my hauntings?
I want respite and not a fleeting bout of merriment
I find peace amidst books
But even the shelfs seem coming at me
I can't reply I'm sorry
I can't show up, I'm sorry
Do not try to find me
I'm clueless I know
Can't control my nerves
Can't say anymore...

8. Espérer

That hot cup of coffee,
Doesn't feel the same anymore,
The warm glare of sun,
Touches me herefore.
You said, "I shall come"
With a conviction--
That I could not reject
I was reassured.
I stepped down a bit,
Looked for a windy cheer,
The leaves were falling.
My coffee is turning cold,
The auburn petals are--
not bright anymore,
We are drifting away.
Your letter hasn't reached me,
Who knows if you wrote?
Saudade wraps me around,
I know you lied to me.
Tears fall down my cheeks,
Making a way to my heart,
I shall still await, because,
Hope is the thing like feathers.

9. Words Et Wars

The harshness of the wind,
The cold blow at par,
I ask "Why are you so angry?"
Their lips are shut,
Those shackles are rusty,
Reds are fading away,
Peace and tranquility,
Are things of the past.
Like the west wind,
Groveling over the edge,
They haunt us--
Their minds numb,
Words don't make a difference.
I was taught "They are our protectors"
I believed so all the while,
Alas! I may have been wrong,
Those straight faces--
aren't familiar anymore.
Barricades and water pipes,
Is what they use?
Yes!! my television screen cried out,
Perhaps, I read those texts wrong.
I know times are different,

Flowers are not only meant for valentines,
They prick you hard,
The longer you hold them.
Can you brush aside your barricades?
Can you open your heart up?
I'm listening,
Can you speak for once?

10. Rose

Scattered all around,
Is my longing for love,
Picking up the pieces
Everyday, I stand.
A caressing touch,
A soft whisper per se,
Talking in silences,
Hearing the unsaid.
A feeling never felt before,
Unfulfilled desires,
Do we stay?
Do we run?
Where do we go?
Underneath a pink sky,
I wait for you,
Will you ever come,
I do not know,
Still, I long for you.
Flowers wilt,
But my rose doesn't,
It has a life of its own,
That the world cannot fathom.
I wish I were you,

Dreaming doesn't cost,
The pink sky is still there,
I am still waiting for you,
You'll come, I know.

11. Rewrite

Have you seen a bird?
Perhaps she is not caged,
But our eyes are illusioned.
When I set out to discover myself,
They stop me right there,
Why do you do that? I ask,
They never give an answer.
One wintry evening,
Under the golden streak of light,
Extended my hands to catch-
Hold that one single cloud,
They say, 'You're mad!'
Just because I laugh at them.
Is this how you label?
My eyes don't wink anymore,
Not sure, if that's my dream,
I want a blank slate,
I want to draw from scratch,
Alas, they don't let me!
My feet don't stay anymore,
They want to fly up high,
Mine tryst is too strong,
They try to stop me,

My grin, they don't understand.
Though retreat is uncertain,
I step up ever too often,
Night's fallin' at the door,
My dreams are for real,
'Useless', is too soon to assume.
Their steps are approaching,
I can hear that clutter,
They cannot keep me back,
because hope is the thing like feathers.
I see the stars now,
They were too far away--
Now I can feel them
The rays of Sun will knock at my door.
Perhaps, I will go with them,
They laugh at me again,
Ask me, are you dreaming?
Today I laugh back at them,
I say,
'Dreams are hopes,
you can never snatch'

12. Life at my door

Thy visionary you see,
Those footfalls you raise,
Downpour from the heavenly praise,
I tap on the crevices.
For you wake up this dawn,
I walk down the lane,
Flickering through my eyes,
Those memories which are mostly sane.
Flashing in front of my eyes,
Like an ocean of dreams,
Pitter patter they sound,
On the window pane.
I wonder and it goes on and on,
I ask them to go back,
But then, they return,
And I ask,
For whose sake you come back?
Why do you knock at my door?
What love do you crave?
Smiling at me, they say,
We give back life.

13. Walking through

Life never pauses,
Brief moments of halts,
A passage to the other side,
Alone we come,
Alone we go,
Meeting several on the sideways,
The skies are bright,
A glimmer of sunshine,
Stepping on a thin line,
Smiling through it all,
A dream of a new beginning.

14. What's at stake?

Upending thoughts,
A chaos within,
Love is disappearing,
and coldness spreads,
A whirlwind of sorts,
Chit chat-chit chat,
The noise engulfs,
Selling and buying,
The market of players,
To be or not to be,
That is the question,
Where are we heading?
What will this lead to?
An emptiness within,
The flares are high,
A road leading nowhere…

15. Special "We Rise"

A vision of the future,
Wings striving to fly high,
Honoring thy assortment,
Standing strong for years,
On the pillars of democracy,
An ardor to grow,
A grit to flourish,
Arise and awake with broad eyes,
Thy country speaketh of equality
Where speech is free,
Where people live together,
Behold! As the Nation unfurls--
Its glory of the mighty dead,
At dawn & dusk.
We rise, we rise, we rise.

www.ingramcontent.com/pod-product-compliance
Lightning Source LLC
Chambersburg PA
CBHW020523160726
47991CB00007B/3099